© **You can live your dreams now**
BY SANDEEP RAVIDUTT SHARMA

# Table of Contents

Foreword .................................................................IV

You can live your dreams now...................................1

© **You can live your dreams now**
BY SANDEEP RAVIDUTT SHARMA

# Foreword

This book provides you with a list of **100** quotes and thoughts about LIFE, churned out by my mind with the consciousness, grace and energy of Shiva Shakti. I'm sure if you keep reading, referring, sharing these thoughts and quotes about LIFE, you may derive inspiration and develop good understanding of various perspectives and facts. Let the world cheer for your achievement. Visualise your victory and make efforts to achieve them.

**"You can live your dreams now with the talk of your actions and use of intelligence."**

I sincerely hope, you will find this book amazing, interesting, rejuvenating, unique and a constant source of Inspiration.

**Thank You and Happy Reading.**

© **You can live your dreams now**
BY SANDEEP RAVIDUTT SHARMA

© **Copyright 2018 Sandeep Ravidutt Sharma - All rights reserved.**
In no way is it legal to reproduce, duplicate, or transmit any part of this document in either electronic means or in printed format. Recording of this publication is strictly prohibited and any storage of this document is not allowed unless with written permission from the publisher. All rights reserved. The information provided herein is stated to be truthful and consistent, in that any liability, in terms of inattention or otherwise, by any usage or abuse of any policies, processes, or directions contained within is the solitary and utter responsibility of the recipient reader. Under no circumstances will any legal responsibility or blame be held against the author / publisher for any reparation, damages, or monetary loss due to the information herein, either directly or indirectly. The author own all copyrights.

**Legal Notice:**
This book is copyright protected. This is only for personal use. You cannot amend, distribute, sell, use, quote or paraphrase any part or the content within this book without the consent of the author or copyright owner. Legal action will be pursued if this is breached.

**Disclaimer Notice:**
Please note the information contained within this book is for motivational, educational and knowledge sharing purpose only. Every attempt has been made to provide the reader accurate, up to date and reliable complete information. No warranties of any kind are expressed or implied. Readers acknowledge that the author is not engaging in the rendering of legal, financial, medical or professional advice. By reading this document, the reader agrees that under no circumstances the author / publisher is responsible for any losses, direct or indirect, which are incurred as a result of the use of information contained within this document, including, but not limited to errors, omissions, or inaccuracies.

If you have further questions, contact on **Tel: +919969256731**
**Email: sandeepraviduttsharma@gmail.com**

© **You can live your dreams now**
BY SANDEEP RAVIDUTT SHARMA

# Dedication

This book is dedicated to **Shiva Shakti** - the epitome of love. Lord Shiva is pure consciousness symbolising the masculine principle. Goddess Shakti symbolises the active feminine energy of Shiva and is synonymously identified with **Tripura Sundari, Sati** or **Parvati**.

These primal principles are also called as PURUSHA representing consciousness and PRAKRITI denoting the nature. Shiva and Shakti are manifestations of the all-in-one divine consciousness. Shiva is the paternal love of God that gives us consciousness, knowledge and clarity. Shakti is the motherly love of God that showers warmth, care and ensures our protection. Shiva and Shakti exist within each of us as the masculine and feminine energy.

To please **Shiva Shakti** praying for the well being, love, happiness, strength, positive energy and success of my readers in their life, I hereby recite the following mantra...

"Sarva Mangala Mangalye Shive Sarvartha Sadhike Sharanye Tryambake Gauri Narayani Namostute"

© **You can live your dreams now**
BY SANDEEP RAVIDUTT SHARMA

# Photo Credits

The beautiful and amazing photograph used for the book cover is clicked by **Nilgün Kanık** from **Turkey**.

You can visit her excellent photo gallery at **Instagram: @nlgncan**

# You can live your dreams now

© **You can live your dreams now**
BY SANDEEP RAVIDUTT SHARMA

*Those who are in the midst of the Sea always crave to touch the shore and the ones on the shore dream of sailing someday. Be happy with what you have but don't stop trying and finding ways to fulfill your dreams.*

© **You can live your dreams now**
BY SANDEEP RAVIDUTT SHARMA

*Tomorrow never come even if you wait for eternity. But hope rests on tomorrow if your present is dark. Keep your hope live forever.*

© **You can live your dreams now**
BY SANDEEP RAVIDUTT SHARMA

*The winner never looks back unless the game is over.*

© **You can live your dreams now**
BY SANDEEP RAVIDUTT SHARMA

*Take a vow to fulfill it and not for some publicity.*

© **You can live your dreams now**
BY SANDEEP RAVIDUTT SHARMA

*Don't waste your time in measuring your success rather make efforts to better it than the last time.*

*Unfulfilled desires can make you restless. Learn to control them with a strong Will else it would start controlling your actions and reactions.*

© **You can live your dreams now**
BY SANDEEP RAVIDUTT SHARMA

*Life struggle will continue even if you win. So why not accept the challenge and make winning a habit.*

© **You can live your dreams now**
BY SANDEEP RAVIDUTT SHARMA

*You don't know much about the world but can always start learning.*

*Not every train you board will take you to your destination. You can reach your destination only when the timing and train are right.*

*When you just think, it's good for you, but when you over think it's fatal. Don't overthink.*

© **You can live your dreams now**
BY SANDEEP RAVIDUTT SHARMA

*The creator always wanted you to be humble and kind. Why else did it give you superior brain and mobility? It was to take care of everyone - human and non-human.*

© **You can live your dreams now**
BY SANDEEP RAVIDUTT SHARMA

*Everyone wants to board fast train in life to reach the destination in time. We tend to forget that train is just the means to reach. The more important aspect which we need to remember is the whole purpose behind the objective, our own ability to reach the destination and lessons learnt during the journey. If we have crushed someone in our quest to board the fast train of life, then even reaching before time will never be satisfactory.*

*Face the reality and accept your mistakes in time. This would give more power and confidence to face challenges of life.*

*Mine the opportunity in time.*

*Aim high in life but stay on ground to realise it.*

© You can live your dreams now
BY SANDEEP RAVIDUTT SHARMA

*Do things your own way and the world will notice you.*

*Life throws surprise at you every second. Be ready to embrace them in time.*

© **You can live your dreams now**
BY SANDEEP RAVIDUTT SHARMA

*Real winners don't even stop to collect their trophies. For them performance only matters.*

*Keep trying to change your approach but never your values.*

© **You can live your dreams now**
BY SANDEEP RAVIDUTT SHARMA

*Flowers smile and shower happiness all around. You can smile and make the world happy.*

© **You can live your dreams now**
BY SANDEEP RAVIDUTT SHARMA

When you tell people about, 'I'm busy', it clearly puts you out of the race to work on prestigious projects. Those who manage their time well will always have enough time for taking up more assignments and responsibilities.

*Failing 99 times is worth, if you could meet Madam opportunity at the hundredth attempt.*

© **You can live your dreams now**
BY SANDEEP RAVIDUTT SHARMA

*Everyone needs motivation but not everyone gets it. If nothing works practice self-motivation.*

*Pick the flowers but remember thorns accompany them by default.*

© **You can live your dreams now**
BY SANDEEP RAVIDUTT SHARMA

*Flowers are liked by millions but only nurtured by few.*

© **You can live your dreams now**
BY SANDEEP RAVIDUTT SHARMA

*When Sky starts falling, you can't save yourself by turning upside down. There are certain situations in your life which you cannot stop from happening. During such hour tie patience to your wrist and keep watching it. The worst time would pass sooner or later.*

*Face the storm of your life with positive attitude, good karma, trust and faith in the almighty God. Remember storm whether big or small is not here to stay. It's just that you are in its way. Hold on to your belief and pray. The storm will pass away making you more stronger than ever before.*

© You can live your dreams now
BY SANDEEP RAVIDUTT SHARMA

*Those who carry the torch of uncertainty even during the day needs to open doors of their mind.*

© **You can live your dreams now**
BY SANDEEP RAVIDUTT SHARMA

*Not every wave could fulfill its dream to meet the Shore, but they keep trying every day.*

© **You can live your dreams now**
BY SANDEEP RAVIDUTT SHARMA

*The relationship cannot be like desert sand which never wants to remain at one place for long. Relationship demands stability of wet soil in a flower pot.*

> © **You can live your dreams now**
> BY SANDEEP RAVIDUTT SHARMA

*Grow enough that you can talk to the Clouds and the Sky.*

© **You can live your dreams now**
BY SANDEEP RAVIDUTT SHARMA

*Winning becomes a routine for excellent performers.*

*Keep the door open wide enough for big time Opportunities to enter.*

© **You can live your dreams now**
BY SANDEEP RAVIDUTT SHARMA

*When you think about benefiting others, you are sure to achieve success. Keep Going.*

*To win every time is desirable but should not hamper your real progress which is mix of both success and failure.*

© **You can live your dreams now**
BY SANDEEP RAVIDUTT SHARMA

*Everything changes its form in this world. Nothing gets destroyed. So why not change ourselves towards a positive and caring form instead of becoming a cruel and destructive weapon.*

© **You can live your dreams now**
BY SANDEEP RAVIDUTT SHARMA

*Those who
are hard working should look
for learning smart work.*

Kind words in harsh tone and harsh words in kind tone are not easy to say unless you are an actor as it comes from your heart and mind. The tone of your voice is the mirror to your true feelings many a times.

© **You can live your dreams now**
BY SANDEEP RAVIDUTT SHARMA

*Everything in life happens for a reason. Don't spend time in finding out the reason, it will automatically appear before you at the right time.*

*Don't get angry just for dominating others. Get angry when freedom is suppressed, respect of your motherland and nature is at stake and corruption rises its ugly head.*

*When someone breaks the rope of trust, even hundreds of knots can't make it one again.*

*Don't read books just to be called as Pandit by others but due to noble intention of acquiring knowledge and benefiting mankind.*

*Step down if you don't seem to be the perfect fit for the role assigned.*

© **You can live your dreams now**
BY SANDEEP RAVIDUTT SHARMA

*Don't quit even if the whole world shouts at you.*

*Everything else around you keeps changing. All you have to do is adapt yourself to the changes and remain relevant.*

*Prayer is more powerful than what everyone thinks. When you pray with your heart, it will be answered. When you pray for others shedding your selfishness, it is sure to be answered.*

© **You can live your dreams now**
BY SANDEEP RAVIDUTT SHARMA

*Don't walk away when the resolution was quite close.*

*Life without Music is no life at all.*

© **You can live your dreams now**
BY SANDEEP RAVIDUTT SHARMA

*It's a great day to start with. Look forward to accomplish a lot.*

© **You can live your dreams now**
BY SANDEEP RAVIDUTT SHARMA

*Dreams turn into reality when common man decides to take over the world with unparalleled grit and determination.*

*Not everyone believes in the creator unless unexpected events and signs start appearing in their lives.*

*Life takes you to place of sorrow and happiness. Your Will power and zeal decide how much time you spend with each of them.*

© **You can live your dreams now**
BY SANDEEP RAVIDUTT SHARMA

*Life sometimes appear as a straight lane and at other times a zig zag path. Learning and testing are life long. You would always hold a temporary driving license.*

*The relationship lasts long when you not only love or like but respect each other.*

*Flowers denote love and happiness.*

© **You can live your dreams now**
BY SANDEEP RAVIDUTT SHARMA

*Real freedom is felt when you can express and do whatever you want.*

*Don't waste time in changing others. The change has to come within your own self.*

© **You can live your dreams now**
BY SANDEEP RAVIDUTT SHARMA

*Mind always questions and heart always accepts.*

*Too much of anything is not good for anyone, whether light or darkness. In both the situation you lose sight.*

*Dark forces laugh throughout the night but quickly gets lost hearing the first footstep of the Sun.*

*Keep Smiling, and you can win the world.*

*Don't remain the slave to defined rules when someone's life is at stake.*

> © **You can live your dreams now**
> BY SANDEEP RAVIDUTT SHARMA

*Don't repeat your mistakes. Discuss solutions in place of problems.*

© **You can live your dreams now**
BY SANDEEP RAVIDUTT SHARMA

*Sometimes you may think and believe that you have given your best, but the glow of achievement seems to be not coming to you. Your destination is defined by your focussed efforts.*

© **You can live your dreams now**
BY SANDEEP RAVIDUTT SHARMA

*If you aim for the Sky at least you will touch the Cloud.*

*Holding grudge against someone is a sureshot way of cultivating happiness. Forgive, and you become richer and happy every minute.*

*Growing tall
makes you noticeable easily
but needs continuous
nurturing.*

*Don't walk way when it's time for you to perform and realise the hope of your near and dear ones.*

© **You can live your dreams now**
BY SANDEEP RAVIDUTT SHARMA

*When one question leads to another, it means you are on the path of revelation and innovation.*

*You may not tolerate inefficiency but first make attempt towards being efficient.*

© **You can live your dreams now**
BY SANDEEP RAVIDUTT SHARMA

*Looking into the mirror makes one feel good. But imagine in the same way where would the mirror go to feel good. The answer is simple the mirror would look into your beautiful eyes.*

© **You can live your dreams now**
BY SANDEEP RAVIDUTT SHARMA

*Don't gamble even if you are sure to win.*

© **You can live your dreams now**
BY SANDEEP RAVIDUTT SHARMA

*All your wishes will be fulfilled by the Lord one day, provided you cross all the hurdles and do enough to see them granted.*

© **You can live your dreams now**
BY SANDEEP RAVIDUTT SHARMA

*Dark clouds carry rain for you still we prefer the white ones. Change your perception; it's not the colour which denotes positive or negative, but it's the intent which can be bad or good.*

© **You can live your dreams now**
BY SANDEEP RAVIDUTT SHARMA

*When you say...it's possible, people may spread the rumor that you have gone crazy. When you prove that you were right they may find ways to eat their words back.*

*Ultimately what do you achieve in life fairly at the end hardly matters to those who were blind throughout the life journey even with two real eyes to see? Nothing can be better than inspiration drawn from a person even when he/she ceases to exist in this world physically.*

*Those who are anxious to know the results are generally the best performers.*

*Everything changes it's form in this Universe.*

© **You can live your dreams now**
BY SANDEEP RAVIDUTT SHARMA

*Real focus blurs out everything else except what you aim for.*

© **You can live your dreams now**
BY SANDEEP RAVIDUTT SHARMA

*Take a walk alone before you talk as it gives you the me time to think and rethink without getting influenced by anyone.*

*Don't gamble with your life by inviting negative vibes through laziness, inconsistent efforts and expression of doubt. All you need to do is fill your mind with motivational and positive thoughts.*

© **You can live your dreams now**
BY SANDEEP RAVIDUTT SHARMA

*Darkness engulfs everything whereas light brings focus back on the chosen ones.*

© **You can live your dreams now**
BY SANDEEP RAVIDUTT SHARMA

*Those who aim to touch the Sky at least succeed in flying kites and fulfill their wish.*

*Not everyone can understand what you mean. Keep trying to make them understand up to a certain point.*

© **You can live your dreams now**
BY SANDEEP RAVIDUTT SHARMA

*Sometimes you feel happy while you lose.*

© **You can live your dreams now**
BY SANDEEP RAVIDUTT SHARMA

*Real friends are those who may not like what you do but to keep you going would comment, 'WELL DONE'.*

*Release the frustration and calm returns.*

*When someone hurts, you don't waste your time in plotting revenge. On the contrary pray to Lord to seek the wellness of the one who has hurt you.*

*Real freedom is felt when you have the power to say, 'no' and is accepted gracefully by others.*

© **You can live your dreams now**
BY SANDEEP RAVIDUTT SHARMA

Each one of us is unique. When God has created us differently... then why do we expect similar behaviour, results and attitude from each other? Each one of us has got a unique signature, style and earth mission. Do things your own way and the world will notice you.

© **You can live your dreams now**
BY SANDEEP RAVIDUTT SHARMA

*Take it easy even if the world gets united to play against you.*

© **You can live your dreams now**
BY SANDEEP RAVIDUTT SHARMA

*Sometimes you spend your lifetime waiting for the right opportunity. Irony is when the right opportunity knocks on your door you don't have the courage to open the door. Don't wait but create opportunities anytime.*

*Facing life challenges requires confidence which stems from knowledge and experience.*

*Understanding each other is critical for the success of a relationship.*

© **You can live your dreams now**
BY SANDEEP RAVIDUTT SHARMA

*Flowers keep smiling and reminding us that even a short life can be beautiful.*

*Yet to find the perfect person on earth. Accept this fact... crave for perfection...but don't wait for perfection.*

*Sometimes you know your fault but still plead ignorance. Its better be truthful to avoid further cover ups.*

*Don't work to record your name in history. Work selflessly and you can create history.*

*Don't remember who you are but what you can do today.*

*Grind your negative thoughts and throw them forever. Attract positivity always.*

www.ingramcontent.com/pod-product-compliance
Lightning Source LLC
Chambersburg PA
CBHW031440210526
45464CB00005B/2277